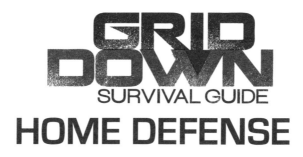

SURVIVAL GUIDE

HOME DEFENSE

AARON IWANCIW

Grid Down Survival Guide
HOME DEFENSE

www.whitman.com

© 2015 Whitman Publishing, LLC
3101 Clairmont Road • Suite G • Atlanta, GA 30329

ISBN: 794842666   EAN: 9780794842666
Printed in the United States of America.

CONTENTS

🏠 INTRODUCTION

As a father, mother, husband, wife, or just plain citizen, each of us has a responsibility to defend ourselves and the Constitution of the United States against foreign and domestic threats. Complacency within our society has allowed our political leadership tip operate unchecked. It has also created a vast domestic dependency on government services and industry for the necessities of life. Ask yourself a very serious question. What would you do right now, at this exact moment in your life, if a crisis struck? You may be at the office, lying in bed, on the porch, or watching television. What would you do if someone breached your home or business to take your valuables or hurt your loved ones? The "fight or flight" instinct within us all would prompt many to fight, and a huge amount of people have responsibility prepared for such a situation by obtaining a firearm for home defense. However, where is your firearm and is it within arm's reach or easily accessible? Did you load your weapon with proper ammunition? Who is in the line of fire and what is beyond your target? How did the intruder get inside your home without you knowing? Are they there to hurt you or just to feed their starving little girl? You must address all of these questions when defending your home.

In our very delicate and dependent society, most merely hold on by a thread until the next paycheck. When we see out neighbors rioting and trampling on another at Black Friday sales or clearing grocery store shelves to hoard food because one inch of snow is on the ground, how will they react in a severe crisis?

INTRODUCTION

A growing number of knowledgeable individuals now prepare for these sudden and inevitable crises. Many mainstream media outlets label these people with demeaning terms. However, I would argue that "being prepared" is one of America's greatest lost attributes.

In our country's founding years, Americans prepared for any kind of storm, drought, flood, or war. They utilized primitive survival and defensive skills while innovating and continually adapting in an ever-changing and unpredictable new world. Defense of the home was critical. No police, 911, or other emergency services existed. Americans had to survive on their own as their preparedness and survival-style of living helped create the greatest nation on Earth.

In today's delicate society, a quick stroke from Mother Nature, a terrorist attack, or an economic crisis like the Great Depression can instantly send us falling right back to the Dark Ages. It only makes sense to remain prepared.

INTRODUCTION

Grid-Down Tip: Remember, when seconds count, the police are only minutes away.

When preparing for a societal breakdown or a grid-down situation, you must role-play every possible scenario in your mind. Go through the "what ifs" and ask yourself the critical questions. Review the topics, tips, tricks, and suggested lists in this book when running through those scenarios to help you become as aware and proficient as possible. Additionally, seek further training and continually increase your defenses and preparations.

As a rule of thumb, no one should consider himself an expert simply because they read a guidebook or watched a TV show on preparedness.

INTRODUCTION

The items, situations, and training in this guidebook will make you aware of what you should know to become proficient. Take what you read in this book and apply the principles and suggestions to your everyday life and preparedness training. The content of this guidebook does not focus on the why or how a collapse might happen, but rather, on preparing to defend your home during any type of grid-down scenario.

INTRODUCTION

🏠 DEFENDING YOUR CASTLE

Whether you find yourself in a disaster scenario or a local gang decides to raid your home during a crisis, your house is your castle, and it must be fortified. In certain situations, you must defend your castle, utilizing any means necessary in order to protect your loved ones and your preparations.

HARD TARGET

First, you need to understand the difference between a hard target and a soft target. Most American suburban homes are soft targets. These houses are easy prey for rioters or looters. Lots of windows and weak wooden doors make for an easy scavenge. Do you remember the story of the three little pigs from childhood? The big bad wolf had a choice

which house he invaded first and, of course, he chose the soft target—the straw house. The brick house was the hard target. You need to turn your house from a target of opportunity into a target of least desire.

Put yourself in an intruder's shoes. Where would you attack? What is the path of least resistance? Find the weak links in your defensive plan and ask other family members or friends to help find vulnerable areas. Look at your neighbor's house. If you were a looter, would you rather raid their house or yours? Looters and burglars tend to be weak-minded individuals and will always take the path of east resistance—the soft target.

DEFENDING YOUR CASTLE

LIGHT AND NOISE DISCIPLINE

The saying, "out of sight, out of mind" definitely applies in a grid down scenario. The power grid requires constant attention to stay operational. When the grid goes down, it can be down for a long period or even indefinitely, and during that time, anything drawing attention to your group, especially the attention of needy individuals or other groups, can be devastating. People will immediately notice that you have "power" as soon as you fire up a lantern or turn on a generator. People will come out of the woods to "borrow." It simply will not make sense to allow everyone to borrow your generator or battery packs. After you turn a few people away, it won't take long for the neighbors to label you as a "hoarder". They may even band together, demand the use of your equipment, and then demand you turn over your food for the "sake of the community." It is best to disguise or hide any noise or light you produce through

physical barriers such as boards or plastic. This may require building a concrete barrier around a generator to dissipate the noise. Also, try not to over utilize lights at night. Do not carelessly utilize a generator to power lights when one candle would adequately light a room. If an attack occurs, you will need your natural night vision to defend your home, and aside from that, any unnecessary depletion of supplies may lead to serious problems later.

DEFENDING YOUR CASTLE

BASIC SITE PREPARATIONS

Gathering site equipment and setting up a defensive type of home may seem like a daunting task, but you can accomplish this starting at any level.

Begin by observing what you have around your property. Unused plywood, wood boards, sheet metal, bolts, and screws all make for simple and effective tools you can utilize for fortifications. You may not necessarily use all of these tools during the preparation phase, but have them on hand and have a plan to use them if the need arises. Get creative. Simple solutions such as dumping a bucket of water on the front stairs during the winter will create an icy deterrent for an intruder in freezing weather. As we discuss in further chapters, don't entirely rely on electronic equipment for your defenses. The grid will be down in certain scenarios, so it's important to employ alternative deterrents

and defenses that don't completely rely on electricity. If you do require electricity, investing in solar panels and a quality battery bank is a worthwhile investment. Immediately following a grid-down crisis, power tools will come in very handy when trying to make final fortifications to your home.

Grid-Down Tip: Modern lithium-ion batteries tend to have a longer shelf life than most other batteries. Rechargeable lithium-ion batteries are readily available and easily recharge with portable solar panel systems.

While developing your initial plan and site preparations, set yourself up for a basic defensive posture and mindset. Your home defenses should constantly evolve and improve over time, but begin with basic burglar protection and develop that into further fortifications as you increase your preparedness level and skill sets.

DEFENDING YOUR CASTLE

🏠 PROPER PRIOR PLANNING

In the military, we utilize the "7 P's" statement: proper prior planning prevents piss poor performance. The fact that you are reading this book indicates you are one step ahead of the game and you understand the need for preparing in case of an unforeseen threat to you or your home. However, every good plan requires secondary and tertiary backup plans, as unforeseen events always occur. Every good plan also requires backup supplies. Examples of backup supplies include backup weapons, ammunition, magazines, water and food supplies, and any fortification materials. You may need more than you think. During a shootout or firefight, law enforcement and military personnel typically expend a significant amount of ammunition. If you find yourself in a similar situation with looters or rioters, you will need ample amounts of

ammo, as well as extra water and food, since your body will burn more calories than normal in a high-stress situation. Try not to keep all your supplies in one area in the event you are overrun. In any case, hope for the best, but prepare for the worst.

Within your group or family, operational security, or OPSEC, should remain an integral part of your planning. OPSEC means keeping your plans to yourself. Unless someone is part of your group, don't discuss details of your defensive plan and don't reveal strengths or weaknesses of your home. During a disaster or grid-down event, you may only have enough food and supplies for you and your family. If this event lasts more than a day or two, the people who know about your plan and preparations will be the first to show up at your doorstep.

PROPER PRIOR PLANNING

A large part of "proper prior planning" must include training in basic defensive skills and tactics. You cannot simply rely on your home defenses as you will inevitably encounter an intruder who successfully breaches your home. Integrate hand-to-hand and firearms training into your plan as a fundamental part of your preparations. Seek out proper training with a professional and practice that training on a regular basis.

PROPER PRIOR PLANNING

⌂THREAT ASSESSMENT: IDENTIFYING OPPOSITION AND DETERRENTS

During a societal breakdown, you will encounter many types of threats. Varying factors cause individuals to act in ways they would not normally act. If faced with hunger, changes in biological and psychological characteristics drive people to more animalistic and violent behavior. You must learn to properly identify types and levels of threats based on a variety of factors. For example, you may encounter a hostile gang or street thug who is out to pillage everything they can find. On the other hand, you may encounter a frustrated father who desperately needs to feed his family. In either case, you must determine the proper threat level as well as the intent. These situations require a high level of moral and ethical calculation. You don't want to regret your actions after the fact.

To properly assess the situation, you should know your own capabilities and limitations of your structure, personnel, weapons, and other preparations. If you are alone in your home with only a few provisions and few defenses, you can't hold your position against an angry armed mob.

Learn to determine the capabilities of the aggressors from quick observation. Identifying opposition and possible deterrents against them requires attention to detail. In some cases, an attacker may be an obvious loner. You may determine the best course of action is to simply ignore him, unless the threat escalates. Remember, having to use force may draw unwanted attention, especially when using loud firearms.

Other threats may involve a small group. Carefully observe their movements and physical capabilities and determine if they possess weapons. Do they appear organized or have an obvious leader? Could you hold out against them if they attack your home? Asking yourself these questions during your preparation phase will help you better assess your own capabilities.

Larger groups pose a higher level of threat. Determine if they are a family, an organized group, a mob, or a militarized unit. Don't forget to determine the intent. Although a large group may impose a high level of threat, this does not mean they have hostile intentions. When defending your home, always use force as a last resort, but don't be afraid to use it when the need arises. The amount of force required is a function of the amount of defenses and security measures you develop. Generally, the

more defenses and deterrents you have, less the likelihood of needing to use force. Developing into a hard target greatly diminishes the need for force.

Ultimately, you want to remain unseen and unbothered in your home or retreat location. Even if an individual or group walks down the street near your home, it's best to remain hidden, as a confrontation will typically end badly for both sides. Never attempt an attack on a person or group that is not directly threatening you. In a disaster or collapse scenario, any type of conflict has much higher risk factors. Hospitals may be useless or non-existent. Limited supplies, lack of power, and few available field-expedient medical providers significantly raise the risks of infections or other life-threatening ailments from even the smallest of injuries.

⌂ DEFENSIVE LAYERS

Within your property, develop three circular layers of defense.

OUTER LAYER

The farthest-reaching layer is the "outer layer", which includes the area between the outermost portion of your property and beyond. This distance will vary for each individual home, but it remains the farthest visible distance where you may encounter a hostile threat. This outer layer typically requires a medium to long-range rifle with an optic. A quality .308 caliber bolt-action rifle is common among defensive experts for this range as well as AR10/AR15-style rifles. The .308 is accurate out to roughly 800 meters. For farther distances, you may require a longer range caliber such as a .300 Winchester Magnum, .338 Lapua Magnum,

or many of the popular 6.5mm cartridges, like 6.5 Creedmoor or .260 Remington. The standard 5.56x45mm NATO/.223 cartridge using the AR-15 platform is typically the best choice for medium range out to 600 meters. In a defensive scenario, keep these weapons in strategic areas of your home for quick access and have a designated marksman focused on the outer layer.

Grid-Down Tip: Always remember the importance of quality optics (scopes) for each of your rifles and make sure they are sighted in on a regular basis. Also, utilize binoculars for spotting threats at a distance.

INNER LAYER

Next is the "inner layer", which includes the area between the outermost portion of the property to the exterior structure of the house. As a potential

threat enters this area, the risk factors rise sharply. Your house now lies within easy range of small arms fire. For this layer, utilize semi-automatic rifles, or in close proximity, shotguns to maximize effectiveness. As we discuss later, early warning devices such as trip flares prove invaluable within this layer.

PERSONAL LAYER

The last defensive layer is the "personal layer," which constitutes the entire area inside your home. Within the personal layer, utilize the shotgun and pistol if intruders breach your home. These short-range weapons prove more effective at close range when you don't want bullets over-penetrating into your internal barricades and thus degrading your defenses or endangering other family or group members in the house.

Security
Avenues of Approach
Fields of Fire
Entrenchment

"Security" has many definitions and comes in many forms, including physical security devices and procedures to increase your situational awareness. Use a systematic approach to implementing your security devices starting with your personal layer and working outward until all of your defensive layers are addressed. It's not always practical to assume you can spend thousands of dollars buying various high-tech devices, nor is it practical to assume power and functionality will remain in place in a grid-down situation. That's why it makes sense to utilize both high-tech and low-tech solutions that are easy to install and can be found around your property or at a local hardware store.

 S.A.F.E.—SECURITY

LOCKS

Many people overlook locks in today's age of complacency. Not all locks are created equal. Ensure you are purchasing high quality steel locks. Secure the locking mechanism using the appropriate screws. It does not make sense to install a high quality lock with half-inch screws. Use quality tempered steel screws that penetrate as far as the type of door or frame will allow. For example, if the thickness of your two materials is 2" then use 1 ¾" screws. It would be even better to have screws long enough to penetrate the studs.

Grid-Down Tip: Do not forget to install high quality external locks on your internal doors. Each time you can slow down an attacker is an opportunity to defeat that attacker or escape.

S.A.F.E.—SECURITY

The use of keyed deadbolts is a great step in the right direction toward personal security. Modern houses are built with many windows and often windowed rear doors. Don't make an intrusion easy by allowing the assaulting force to simply break a pane of glass, reach in, and unlock the door so they can walk right in. An important note to keep in mind for children is to ensure your appropriately aged and capable young ones are able to access any keys required to leave or escape the home. Also, remember that a lock is only as strong as the door and frame.

SIMPLICITY

Simplicity is key with security. A lock can be any mechanism used to fasten or secure doors or windows. Preferably, the mechanism operates by a key, but simply screwing your door shut or using a chain lock can slow an assault tremendously. Even wedging a plank or board behind a door provides a simple solution.

 S.A.F.E.—SECURITY

EARLY WARNING DEVICES

Given a full social or economic collapse, unless you have a retreat location with established security, you will not have adequate 24-hour guard duty. There will also be significant responsibilities amongst your family simply to acquire and maintain life-providing essentials. Therefore, adequate early warning devices are a must. These devices may consist of high-tech or low-tech options. The trick is to utilize simple solutions and continually improve. In this section, you'll read about just a few options commonly found around the house or easily ordered online.

EXTERIOR ALARMS

Any area outside of your personal layer can be equipped or monitored by utilizing exterior alarms. These alarms can be visual, audible, or both. For example, in the military, we used trip flares, which are very reliable and simple devices, that are easy to set and very effective. When the approaching force realizes they have activated an early warning flare that shoots up into the air, the mental impact is demoralizing. However, trip flares are not always available to the public.

Examples of exterior alarms include:

Wind Chimes

Use: inner layer near the structure attached to trip wires to cause maximum noise

Advantages: simple low-vis (low visual signature) items that won't turn heads

Disadvantages: blows in the wind, so it can throw false alarms

Driveway Sensors

Use: inner/outer layer, used where properly funneled traffic will set it off

Advantages: wired units have direct connection to the structure and wireless units can be used at a distance

Disadvantages: sensors run on power, so even battery-powered options will require solar recharges

Surveillance Cameras (Exterior)

Use: camera systems are force multipliers used to observe avenues of approach or remote assets such as wells or cellars

Advantages: increases awareness and provides additional time to build your response to threats

Disadvantages: requires power and relies on the person assigned to watch the camera

Game Cameras

Use: these can be used as extreme remote observation posts used to observe patterns

Advantages: portable and discrete

Disadvantages: battery operated and not real-time, while non-wireless units require physical retrieval of the data

Wire Triggers

Use: wire triggers can be strung across an area of approach and attached to just about anything that makes noise

Advantages: readily available

Disadvantages: can be detected and avoided

INTERIOR ALARMS

It is helpful to have internal security alarms or monitors in case an intruder enters your structure. The purpose of these systems is to monitor the movement and make you aware of an advancement.

Camera Systems (Interior)

Camera systems are very useful, but require power. Baby monitors are very inexpensive ways to momentarily monitor noise and movement. However, since they require power, they are not the most practical form of monitoring in a grid-down scenario, especially over extended periods.

Door Chimes

Door chimes are typically long lasting, battery operated devices that not only provide you with an early warning, but may also "spook" an intruder trying to discretely open a door.

It is important to use your ingenuity. Anything that alerts you of movement within your structure can be a form of security. Stacking toys or even pots and pans by or near entry points can be a great way to increase awareness of discrete entry attempts.

Security
AVENUES OF APPROACH
Fields of Fire
Entrenchment

An avenue of approach is a route used by an attacking force leading to your home or leading to key terrain in the path to your home. Go over in your mind how and where you would attack your own home. Blocking or directing avenues of approach will require your ingenuity in developing obstacles to function as funnels or deterrents. It is extremely important to place these obstacles in strategic locations without creating cover or shooting positions for the intruding force.

WHERE WILL THEY COME FROM?

There are essentially two ways an attacking force will approach your position–by foot or vehicle. The key is to make an approach difficult and to guide the approach into an area that is strategically advantageous to

you while simultaneously strategically disadvantageous to the attacker. Think of ways to force the attacker into places where you can focus maximum firepower.

Your driveway is one of the most likely routes for a vehicle attack. Placing any immovable object or destructive device within that path will assist in stopping or impeding the rapid advance of any force. Depending on the layout of the area to the left and right of the driveway, use items such as logs, trees, cinder blocks, even lawn mowers and other vehicles. Do not forget that a deep enough ditch is almost impossible to cross without the proper equipment.

Almost every modern structure has sidewalks leading up to porches and decks. It is a common habit to follow those up to the point of entry. Make the approach difficult by utilizing any form of wire, boards, grease, ice (in cold environments), or even planters to obstruct or impede progress. Anything that forces the attacker's focus off of the attack or causes injury will help to provide the critical time needed to respond to an assault. Remember, do not use an obstacle or obstruction the intruder could use as cover.

HARDENING THE AVENUE OF APPROACH

Porch

Grease the rails and steps of your front and back porch. Take the chains off your swing set and run them from rail to rail about waist high. Screw a board securely across the porch entry.

Decks

Most back doors with a deck are elevated. Remove the planks and make it harder to climb. You can then use the planks to secure other entry points. Get underneath the deck and weaken the planks by using a saw to cut through the majority of the board. Place obstacles, such as chairs on the stairs to act as a deterrant.

Windows and Doors

Having precut plywood of any thickness or strength will offer a tremendous amount of security. Unless you live in an area where you plan to routinely apply and remove these panels, plan to nail or screw them directly into the framing. Keep in mind, any steel pieces of aluminum roofing panels, wire fencing, or even fireproof coatings on the outer layer will provide additional protection from intruders. Other options for securing your door may include:

- Plywood or wooden planks
- Eyebolts and rebar
- Prop bars (floor to door)
- Screws and nails
- Inward/outward opening doors

 S.A.F.E.—AVENUES OF APPROACH

Grid-Down Tip: It is important to note that you may be forced to leave due to an overwhelming attacking force or simply by superior firepower. Make sure that you have the ability to quickly exit your property.

Fences

Fences can be the first deterrent when hardening an avenue of approach and may also serve as the outermost layer of security. Fences are useful for two things: slowing down attackers and guiding movement. Making yourself a hard target begins by making it difficult to enter your outer layer. Consider the following example. House "A" has no visual signs deterring potential threats from simply walking up to the front or back door. Conversely, house "B" has a fence, a deep ditch, boards on the windows, and various other signs of defense. Which one would you want to walk up to?

If you decide to put up a fence, take into consideration the type you

S.A.F.E.—AVENUES OF APPROACH

would like to install. Home Owners Associations, group agreements, or the function of the fence itself will sometimes limit the design of the fence. A tall chain-link fence works well but can be unattractive in a front yard. White picket fences may look nice, but will not offer much of a deterrent to an intruder. The same is true of decorative fences which typically require very little effort to simply walk through. If you want a nice look, but need the function of something more secure, just overbuild the fence. In other words, use an aestheic design but build it with sturdier, more heavy duty materials. Use 6x6 posts and 4x4 cross beams with 2x4 sections. You may even want to cut those sections to a very sharp point and go up to at least chest height. Most people will not want to climb something like that and can't easily break through it, but this type of fence will still look attractive.

S.A.F.E.—AVENUES OF APPROACH

A common tactic is to outfit privacy fences with electric fence capability. You can place the electric cable just out of sight on the inner side of the fence. Though not a lethal deterrent, it may turn away the occasional wanderer, which achieves the goal of any fence, to aid in security by either deterring or redirecting an intruder.

Security
Avenues of Approach
FIELDS OF FIRE
Entrenchment

"Fields of fire" refers to the areas around your property that need to be covered by individual or team based fire. These areas are usually designated after assuming a defensive barricaded or entrenched position. Utilizing proper fields of fire is extremely important when

defending your home in a grid-down scenario. After you have determined the most likely avenues of approach from an attacking force, those areas will be included in your fields of fire. Within the larger fields of fire, each individual or team should have a separate sector of fire. Sectors of fire are usually "pie" shaped and designate lateral and forward limits of your fire. You will have to determine a left and right lateral limit for each position, a designated spot or marker that limits both the direction of fire. For an indoor example, the forward frame of a door in the living room to your left can be your left lateral limit. You may designate that as your limit because you know you have positioned another friendly barricade just on the other side of that door. Without these limits, randomly firing in the direction of an intruder may cause devastating injuries to family or group members located behind your target. You can also use other types of wall markers inside the room to designate your left and right

lateral limits within your sector of fire. Wall markers may include pictures on the wall, a light switch, or simply painting or marking lines or dots on the wall. Again, know what lies beyond your wall markers so that you don't shoot at unintended people, valuables, or defenses. Draw out a specific diagram of your home, showing specific markers and sectors of fire. Make sure to cover every area of your home or property. Sectors of fire should always be mutually supporting, which means the pie-shaped sectors should overlap. This overlap is typically referred to as interlocking sectors of fire, which will decrease the risk of any gaps in your defenses.

The most effective way to establish fields and sectors of fire is to walk through an attack scenario as an attacker. Determine how and where you would attack and plan to cover those areas with defensive firepower.

S.A.F.E.—FIELDS OF FIRE

FIRING POINTS

While establishing your sectors of fire, you must specify specific firing points (shooting positions) within each sector. Simply put, a firing point is a specifically designated shooting position in a room or hallway, with its sector of fire being comprised of the set range and direction of fire from that particular position. Predetermined firing points along with interlocking sectors of fire create an ideal defensive position that limits friendly fire and maximizes enemy casualties. This also helps to prevent any degradation to your defenses.

Identifying proper firing points is a very important aspect of maintaining a solid defense. Depending on your location, firing points may be inside or outside of your home. These positions should give you the best possible line of sight and provide cover and concealment. Stock these positions with proper supplies to support the shooter.

Grid-Down Tip: The difference between cover and concealment. Many people oftentimes confuse cover with concealment. In the heat of battle, you'll need to know the difference. Concealment is anything that visually obstructs observation by the opposing unit, whereas cover is anything that provides protection against enemy fire.

Firing points need to be predetermined and assigned to the right individuals. Post the best shooters at firing points that may require a longer distance shot. Hand-to-hand fighting experts should be posted inside the home in case of a successful intrusion by attackers. Determining the location of your firing points and having a plan to utilize them is extremely important to your overall defensive plan.

Ensure proper fields and sectors of fire by making sure firing points have the most coverage possible. Individuals in a firing point should have clear visibility of their sector of fire. They should also have visibility of other team members within an overlapping sector of fire on each side. Firing points should always support one another. You may have to defend multiple buildings on your property, in which case your firing points will become even more important.

Utilizing elevation when setting up firing points affords the benefits of increased observation and more optimal fields of fire. Second and third story windows supply vantage points and firing angles that aren't available at ground level. However, lower level firing points provide for very effective grazing fire which is extremely effective against large attacking forces. Grazing fire was originally used as a term describing when military machine

S.A.F.E.—FIELDS OF FIRE

gunners lay down fire parallel to the ground to cut off a ground assault. In a scenario where you are defending against a large movement of attackers, your ground level defenders will want to fire as quickly as possible at all targets of opportunity. By utilizing grazing fire, even if your team members miss their intended targets, the hope is that the travel of the bullet will be no more than one meter off the ground, allowing for the possibility of the bullet to hit another attacker farther back in the assault.

Firing points need to be barricaded and reinforced to protect the defender from enemy fire. Use anything at your disposal to make this happen. For example, empty a filing cabinet, turn it on its side, and fill it with rock or dirt from your driveway. Bags of cement or sand are also very useful for protection. While reinforcing your firing points, ensure you are not limiting your effective range of fire with the placement of your barricades and other reinforcements. Always maintain an adequate field of fire.

 S.A.F.E.—FIELDS OF FIRE

FOLIAGE AND OBSTRUCTIONS

Natural and manmade obstructions can affect the shooters ability to engage targets. Remove all line-of-sight obstructions in order to allow for effective enemy engagement. Study the sector of fire and personally inspect each firing point to ensure the removal of all obstructions. These obstructions may include porch railings, shrubs, and lower level tree limbs. Although it may seem like you can easily shoot though these items, even a blade of grass can have dramatic effects on the long-range accuracy of a single bullet. You must be able to clearly see the threat you want to eliminate. Properly defending your home requires good line-of-sight observation.

TERRAIN FEATURES

From each firing point, all shooters must identify terrain features within their sectors of fire, as these features can aid in the advancing of an enemy force. Specifically, shooters need to note key micro-terrain features. Micro-terrain refers to small ground features, such as ditches, fences or shrubs, which can be used to conceal an advancing attacker and typically provide cover or concealment. Micro-terrain features do not show up on typical maps of the area, as they are smaller and less significant than large buildings or roadways. However, micro-terrain is incredibly significant when developing a defensive position, as you must know these terrain features to properly adjust fields and sectors of fire. Also, it's important to note any defilades, which are man-made or natural objects that render your weapon system ineffective against the enemy and typically provide a high level of protection against direct gunfire.

RANGING TARGETS

Now that you've established your shooting positions, provided cover and concealment, and identified your defilades and micro-terrain, it is time to identify the range or distance to your targets. Don't wait for a battle to break out before you range the distance to potential target areas. For instance, know that the end of your driveway is 300 meters and that a yard planter is 50 meters. If an attacker comes near any of your pre-ranged terrain features, you will know the approximate distance to the target. This will allow for proper target acquisition and quick range adjustments without having to rely on range finders and batteries. If needed, adjust your firearm's sights to the most probable entry point onto your property. Once you know the ranges and micro-terrain within your sector of fire, write them down on a fire plan sketch.

S.A.F.E.—FIELDS OF FIRE

FIRE PLAN SKETCH

One of the best and most practiced ways to ensure everyone understands their sector of fire is to have them individually draw it out on paper. Military personnel frequently call this drawing a fire plan sketch. The fire plan sketch should include a drawing of your shooting position and your immediate area. If you are defending a position outside, your fire plan sketch should include a drawing of your shooting position, your sector of fire with left and right lateral limits, any micro-terrain, distances to probable enemy approach locations, and any other notable hills, shrubs, large rocks, vehicles, or terrain features. If defending a position indoors, your fire plan sketch should include a drawing of your shooting position, your sector of fire with left and right lateral limits, a top-down layout view of the structure or home, and any key internal features. Any fire plan sketch should also include the positions and sectors of fire of any other

team or group members. In some cases, your shooting position may be inside the house, but at a door or window with a firing port. For this scenario, you will need to include indoor and outdoor features on your fire plan sketch.

ALTERNATE FIGHTING POSITIONS

You must always identify both a primary and an alternate fighting position for each defensive shooting position. When defending your home, make sure you are defending in depth, utilizing your fallback locations. If your primary fighting position becomes compromised when someone breaches your outer perimeter, and you are unable to push the enemy back, an alternate fighting position becomes necessary.

Security
Avenues of Approach
Fields of Fire
ENTRENCHMENT

We all remember the history book pictures and the fairytale drawings of the castle and the moat. The moat was one the earliest forms of entrenchment. Imagine how hard it would be to attack a castle with a 20-foot deep moat extending all the way to 40-foot high stone walls. When in use, those entrenchments forced any attackers into a fatal funnel like a bridge or main door. In modern times, a fatal funnel is any terrain or man-made structure that consolidates a dispersed force into pre-designated areas of concentrated fire. To repel a group of attackers, force the attackers into any form of a fatal funnel. Whether you fabricate the funnel with large immovable objects or you utilize an existing funnel like a hallway or doorway, use it to your advantage.

S.A.F.E.—ENTRENCHMENT

FORTIFICATIONS

Fortifying your home with physical objects is a requirement for any type of defensive posture. Doors and windows are the first entry points most will use to enter your home. Lock, reinforce, barricade, or even screw the doors and windows shut. Make it as arduous as possible to enter your home using any means necessary. You must not forget about the back or side door. Back and side doors are usually the most difficult to reinforce due to thin and cheaply made modern doors, many of which have glass panes. Many modern houses typically have windows throughout the back section of the house. Fortify these areas with plywood, steel sheets, wooden planks, or even a tarp if that is all you have. Do not forget that you must be able to get out of your fortified house, even if injured.

S.A.F.E.—ENTRENCHMENT

DOORS

When you start with your basic site fortifications, begin with the doors. The first thing to do is to inspect your door. Is it in good condition and made of sturdy materials? You are in far better shape if you have a steel or solid oak door. If you have planked or paneled doors, try to replace them as your budget allows. Make your door as strong as possible and as uncommon as possible. For example, there are a large number of trained military and law enforcement personnel who will get just as hungry as civilians in a total collapse scenario. Anyone trained in breaching knows to compromise door hinges with a shotgun blast. The hinges are usually located about a foot from the bottom and top of the door and at center height. Imagine how long it would take someone to figure out you have four or five hinges instead of the standard two or three. That extra minute or two gives you and your family extra time to either escape or eliminate the threat trying to enter your home.

S.A.F.E.—ENTRENCHMENT

If you decide to replace a door, remember to never put the hinges on the outside of the door as this would render it useless as a defense. An attacker could simply pop out the pins and remove the door from the frame.

WINDOWS

Windows are the second most common entry point for non-military breaching. Be prepared to remove all the glass from the windows and insert your precut plywood or steel if the need arises. Ensure you insert firing ports in those strategic locations. To create a firing port, cut a small, vertical slit in the plywood or steel over the window. This slit should be large enough to maneuver your rifle left to right, but small enough so you are not exposed to gunfire. For example, if you have a window on your front porch that supports observation of the front door, you will want to defend that door through the window firing port.

Knowing your angles and having predetermined sectors of fire helps create a strong defense. Have a friend or family member stand at the doors and windows and see if you have proper angles and sectors of fire from your position inside. During an attack, refrain from getting close to your windows as much as possible unless they are armored, as many attackers are going to shoot at the windows.

Grid-Down Tip: Securing two pieces of plywood or steel on both sides of a window will allow you to fill that cavity with rock, sand, or dirt. This will help dissipate a bullet's energy and break up the core when penetrating. (Just remember that this defense will also impede bullets from the inside as well.)

S.A.F.E.—ENTRENCHMENT

CRAWL SPACES AND ATTICS

Crawl spaces and attics can also be used as unexpected fire support positions, but they have several disadvantages. Both provide limited vantage points, making a moving target difficult to follow. Crawl spaces and attics also present a disadvantage if you're forced to abandon your position in a hurry due to the limited access to each of them.

FORCE BARRICADES

Always have a plan in the event attackers breach your defenses and get inside your home. A determined attacker with the right tools will eventually get through. Depending on the strength and value of your door, it may not be worth letting them destroy it. You may want to leave it open if you know the group advancing has ill intent. This easy entry invites all attackers to enter together, concentrating them in a small area and making them easier targets. Control their movement by creating force barricades located at inner doors and hallways. Again, most attackers will take the path of least resistance. Create force barricades by using plywood or other objects like tables, chairs, couches, and even box springs from under your mattresses. This can help to funnel attackers into hallways and rooms that become kill zones where your defensive forces can unleash massive amounts of firepower.

Building barricades within your home is only limited by your imagination and ingenuity. When the world gets to the point where you're barricading your home, comfort and luxury are far less important. Use anything and everything that will slow down an attacker. Inner doors such as bathroom, closet, and cabinet doors can be removed from their hinges and used as barricade materials and obstacles.

For exterior barricades, natural terrain features can be some of the best forms of defense. Unfortunately, not all of us have the advantage of natural barriers. The use of masonry or wood planters can provide a tremendous amount of protection from gunfire and other threats, when planters are strategically placed. Position heavy planter boxes or pots in front of garage doors, low windows, and other doors as a barrier to gunfire and even approaching vehicles.

Anything that slows movement will give you the extra split second you may need to react and appropriately defend your life and home. Gain as many split seconds as you can by thinking outside the box and utilizing everything in and around your home to support your entrenchments.

 S.A.F.E.—ENTRENCHMENT

⌂ ADDITIONAL DEFENSES & SUPPLIES

BACKUP STAGING

At this point in the process, every person should ideally be armed and ready to fight at all times. However, nothing ever goes quite as planned. In a grid-down situation, many things can catch you off guard. Make sure each firing point is properly stockpiled with food, water, loaded magazines, weapons, and fire extinguishers, as well as proper medical supplies. Here is a quick list of items to stage at each fighting point.

- Loaded pistol and rifle magazines
- Shotgun and other weapons
- Containers of purified water, preferably with drink tubes
- Individual trauma kits

- Foods that are quickly and easily consumed
- Waste receptacle for using the restroom

You never know how much time you will spend at a barricaded position, so it is important to have everything you need properly staged.

 Grid-Down Tip: Most importantly, keep your weapons on your body or within an arm's reach at all times. You cannot defend anything without your weapons.

SAFE ROOMS

Safe rooms do not have to be underground concrete bunkers. Though ideal, these setups are not always feasible. A safe room is your main point for coordination and defense. This may serve as your headquarters and your fallback point of absolute last stand defense. Preferably, it is

 ADDITIONAL DEFENSES & SUPPLIES

in a central location with the least amount of windows. Keeping the safe room centralized means your fighters out at the firing points can converge on the safe room with equal amounts of effort and risk. Having as few windows as possible will reduce the risk of observation from any attacking forces. This might just be a hallway at the center of your home, if that is your only option. Wherever you decide to put your safe room, make sure you have a written plan for insertion and extraction. You always want to be able to easily get in and out if the need arises. You will want to maintain a bulk of your supplies at this location. Some of those supplies should include:

- Food and water
- Medical supplies
- NBC (nuclear, biological, and chemical) protection
- Ammunition/loaded magazines
- Fire extinguishers

 ADDITIONAL DEFENSES & SUPPLIES

FIRE PROTECTION

Gangs and looters often use fire as a means of intimidation. During the winter seasons, the use of fire and other heaters for warmth will substantially increase the risk of accidental fires. In a grid-down situation, the police and fire services could be severely disrupted, thus limiting their ability to respond to residential fires. Fire extinguishers are an absolute must in every room and at every fighting position. Do not forget to position multiple extinguishers in your attic and crawlspace. Residential houses typically contain many flammable and easily burnable items, such as wood flooring, carpet, beds, dressers, and closets full of clothes. Flammable items such as paints, gasoline canisters, oils, and even trash pose a serious fire hazard when stored inside your garage. As you begin to prepare your home for defense, take into account your flammable possessions and remove them. If a firing position is indoors on top of carpet, remember to lay down a non-flammable material so your spent brass casings don't set your carpet ablaze. The use of fireproof foam greatly enhances your home defenses against fire. Go the extra mile when you have the supplies and means to make improvements to your home defenses, particularly with fire protection.

COMMUNICATION

Having the ability to communicate in a defensive scenario is key to success. You will need to be able to communicate with your team not only to relay the enemy's position, but also to relay your own. Few people live in homes that allow for simple communication. It is important to know when your family members are moving from primary to secondary firing points and when you can safely engage intruders. Communication doesn't have to be high-tech radios and headsets. Simple yelling can

 ADDITIONAL DEFENSES & SUPPLIES

work, but this will drastically reduce your effectiveness. Quality two-way radios with headsets add a significant force multiplier to your defenses. You will need batteries and a way to charge the radios, but this is a worthwhile investment. If possible, use brevity codes and acronyms so that you're not giving away your action and location in case the attackers also have radios on the same frequency. The use of brevity codes or acronyms shortens the amount of time used to relay a message. Since it is shorthand, this adds a small amount of security when talking over openly transmitting radios or verbally. When planning to use brevity codes, make sure everyone in your group familiarizes themselves with all of the codes and rehearses regularly. Rehearsing your communication plan is critical. In an active firefight, it is extremely difficult to hear, especially when shooting inside of a building. If you engage in a firefight without earplugs, you will usually experience temporary deafness. However, if

 ADDITIONAL DEFENSES & SUPPLIES

you are wearing ear protection, that protection may hinder your ability to communicate. 3M makes a wide variety of combat earplugs allowing for verbal communication while still providing impulse protection from gunfire.

WEAPONS

A weapon can be any type of tool or object a person can use for defensive or offensive purposes. When defending your home as a group, it is important to take into consideration the type and uniformity of all your weapons. If each group member carries the same basic weapons, they will be able to share the same ammunition, magazines, and spare parts. Also, if a member needs to use another member's weapon, they will already be familiar with the functions if they have the same weapon systems. In a grid-down scenario, you will undoubtedly encounter attackers with firearms. As the old adage goes, "Don't bring a knife to a gunfight." The only way to come out on top is to maintain superior firepower. Ensure that you and your group maintain ample amounts of ammunition for each caliber. Properly sight in each firearm and know the range and limitations of each gun. Of course, engaging in a firefight is a last resort, as both sides will almost always suffer casualties.

During a grid-down situation, attackers can come at all hours of the night and day. All members of your unit should carry not only their primary weapon system, but also their secondary weapon at all times. Situations will arise when you will find yourself in need of more firepower than just your primary weapon. You may also find yourself in a situation where it is faster to change weapons than to change magazines. Having the right weapon with additional ammunition preloaded into its proper

ADDITIONAL DEFENSES & SUPPLIES

magazine is extremely important. Stage your long rifles and extra M4/AR-style rifles at the exterior firing positions. Keep your extra shotguns and pistols at your back-up fighting positions.

Typically, a primary weapon system allows a shooter to defend from a distance. Your secondary would be the weapon used within a shorter range or as a backup. As Marines, our primary weapons were our M16A4s or our M4s, and our secondary weapons were pistols, knives, or bayonets. A law enforcement officer's primary weapon may be his pistol at his hip and his secondary could be his compact pistol at his ankle. Keep in mind, your secondary weapon may just be a bayonet or pocket knife, but at some point, your primary weapon will go down. Given enough time and enough rounds, your primary weapon will fail, and having a secondary line of defense can determine the difference between life and death. Make sure you have a secondary weapon,

ADDITIONAL DEFENSES & SUPPLIES

and train with both your primary and secondary weapon systems. The weapons you or your team carry are not nearly as important as the proficiency level at which you can wield each of them. Attend professional shooting classes and practice on a regular basis.

TOOLS

Many tools and supplies are easily overlooked and under prioritized. Take inventory of what you have on hand. Know what you need to scavenge or purchase prior to a grid-down event. It would be a shame to have a rechargeable screw gun but no working battery charger and a very limited screw assortment. Ensure you keep plenty of screws and nails on hand. Power tools are extremely helpful in a disaster scenario, but they must either be recharged with solar power or you must have generators to run them. Don't forget that you may also need automotive

tools to repair vehicles. These tools typically vary from the standard sizes. Also, chainsaw and handsaw importance should not be overlooked. If you're building anything with wood, you will need proper cutting tools. A chainsaw is also very useful for procuring firewood. These saws are also very useful for cutting holes into walls between your rooms for ease of access, which speeds up your defensive and extraction response times. However, always keep basic, manual hand tools on hand in the event you run out of gasoline or electricity.

EXTRA MATERIALS

Wood

Plywood and wood boards are some of the easiest building materials to work with in construction and entrenching. Their weight to strength ratio makes them perfect for home fortifications. Always make sure you purchase pressure treated lumber when making your selection at the lumberyard or at your local hardware store, as this wood will widthstand the elements far more successfully.

Duct Tape & Plastic

Duct tape and plastic can play a significant role in the preparation of your home for a defensive scenario. They can be used for water gathering, sealing off rooms to control airflow, distraction devises, or obstacles for intruders. Dark plastics and duck tape can also be used to control light emission from your home at night. This will help to maintain a low visibility signature.

ADDITIONAL DEFENSES & SUPPLIES

Other Supplies

These are just a few items to have on standby for assisting in security preparations:

- Heavy mil plastic
- Wood planks
- Plywood sheets
- Nails, screws, and washers in assorted sizes
- Hammers
- Shovels
- Work gloves
- Philips and flathead screwdrivers, of varying sizes
- Duct tape
- Knife sharpening system

MEDICAL

Be prepared to treat every medical incident that will arise in a societal breakdown. Start by identifying your major medical threats such as trauma, burns, and broken bones. While conducting your planning, consider all current medical prescription needs.

The level of treatment capability will depend on four things: preparation, money, skills, and time. You can have all the money in the world to buy supplies, but without the proper training, they are pretty much useless. You might have the money and the training, but if you didn't take the time to organize, properly store the supplies, or teach others, you could find yourself being the one injured with no one to administer medical attention. However, all households will need some basic first aid essentials regardless of your wealth or skill set.

 ADDITIONAL DEFENSES & SUPPLIES

BASIC FIRST AID AND TRAUMA

You must not overlook the importance of having a basic first aid kit. The amount of work and preparations required for daily living in a grid down situation will increase tremendously. Everything from gathering water to burning the trash will take more time and effort. All this extra work will dramatically raise the likelihood of injury. Trauma care for individuals should match the level of training within your group. The North American Rescue Tactical Operator Response Kit contains a great mix of items for an individual trauma kit.

- 1 x Bag (TORK)
- 4 x Bear Claw Nitrile Glove (2 pr.)
- 1 x Nasopharyngeal Airway 28F with Lubricant
- 1 x HyFin Chest Seal Twin Pack

ADDITIONAL DEFENSES & SUPPLIES

- 1 x ARS Needle Decompression Kit (14 G x 3.25 in.)
- 1 x C-A-T (Combat Application Tourniquet)
- 1 x Z-Fold Combat Gauze
- 1 x S-Rolled Gauze (4.5 in. x 4.1 yd)
- 1 x ETD 6 in. Emergency Trauma Dressing
- 1 x Trauma Shears

Your group's medical supplies should constantly improve and evolve. Maintain a list of medical supplies and any expiration dates for any medications. A family preparing to survive social disorder must be able to protect itself against any type of threat. Sometimes that threat may come in the form of chemical or biological attacks. Although typically not life-threatening, CS gas (tear gas) is the most prominent threat. Gangs may use CS gas stolen from law enforcement personnel for looting. The ability to accurately engage oncoming attackers can be devastatingly

compromised while being affected by CS. Invest in quality gas masks and surgical face masks for these situations.

KEEP IT CLEAN

Part of protecting your home is cleaning it. Remove all unnecessary objects that may present fire or trip hazards. This will allow for easier defense and reduce the risk of fire from both everyday use and during an intrusion. Continually clean your home to reduce the risk of bacteria, mold, or infections, all of which are more threatening with limited medical resources during a grid-down scenario. Once the grid goes down and people begin to get hungry, they will look anywhere and everywhere for food, which may include trash cans. If hungry neighbors resort to going through your trash in search of food, your empty freeze-dried food packets they find will inform them of your supply stash and may prompt an attack on your group. As a solution, retain your trash or burn it if that is a discrete option.

 ADDITIONAL DEFENSES & SUPPLIES

⌂ ESCAPE ROUTES

FALLING BACK

You have been breached and you can't hold. It sounds melodramatic to say you will "fight to the death," but in a life or death scenario, each of us would resort to that. The goal should be to live and fight for as long as you can. Eliminating ten targets in a glorious battle only to die in the end does little good for your family or group. Strategically eliminating five and then coming back to get another five successfully has much more long term benefit. Have a plan for falling back when you find yourself with your personal layer breached. Notice: I don't say retreat. Fall back to a more advantageous position. This will increase your likelihood of overall success. Rehearse this plan every time you train. Do not underestimate the value of practice and communication. If you are in a group with

untrained individuals, they are going to look to you or the leader of the group for guidance. They will be scared and may fall back too soon. Make sure they know who will make the determination of when to fall back or what predetermined situations must occur prior to falling back. It is important to have an established order of command so that when a leader is killed, the entire group knows who is next in line to take charge.

CACHE SITES

When you and your group choose to fall back, having the proper equipment is essential to survival. Every pilot and every special forces operator has an "E&E" bag. This escape and evasion bag holds just the essentials—food, water, ammo, survival kit, and communications. Sometimes in the heat of the moment, you or others may not be able to carry or get to this bag. Therefore, it is necessary to have cache

sites nearby or positioned along the route to an evacuation point. Just remember, from this point, you must stay mobile. Depending on where you're going, you may need your pack to be light for fast and short travels or you may need a pack equipped for a month long trek across the state.

GETTING OUT ALIVE

There may come a time when getting out is your only realistic option. Let's say you have a defensive group of eight individuals. If an armed force of over twenty rioting attackers is coming directly toward your location and your outer layer defensive engagements are not slowing them down or turning them around, it is time to get out. Realistically, regardless of how fortified your home is, time and energy is not on your side. Eight people simply cannot stay awake longer than twenty can.

Eight people cannot pull triggers as fast as twenty can. It is important to remember that this is not the movies and heroes don't always fight off the enemy and live to get the medal. If you have kids, or even if it's just you and your spouse, take into consideration what you see, determine the attacker's intent, and make a decision. I will say again: MAKE A DECISION. Do not wait until it is too late. It is your duty to survive and fight another day. Do not opt to die killing six of the twenty and leave your wife without a husband or your kids without a father. You may die leaving them to face the rest of the surviving attackers alone. If it looks like you are severely outnumbered, simply pack up, get out of there, and re-engage on your own terms. Please don't misinterpret this section. I'm not saying to run from every fight. Just pick your battles with an eye toward long-term survival—your constant focus in a grid-down scenario.

ESCAPE ROUTES

🏠 AUTHOR'S BIO

Aaron Iwanciw is a combat veteran with eight years of Marine Corps Infantry experience. He joined the Marine Corps with a passion to fight on the frontlines in defense of our great country. He grew up in the foothills of Middle Tennessee, shooting with his father and attending scout meetings, consistently learning the value of preparedness. As a young boy, Aaron knew he wanted to be a Marine. While many options were available to him, he specifically selected the Marine Corps Infantry. The honest reality of war became personal only a few years later while conducting military force protection operations and countless combat patrols in Iraq. While conducting those duties, he was witness to the consequences of individuals becoming complacent and dependent on government for all they have, making them part of a societal collapse. Observing the effects of chemical changes within desperate and hungry individuals of the populous was life changing. Witnessing frustration turning to aggression and aggression turning to violence changed Aaron's way of thinking forever. Now honorably discharged from the military, Aaron leads his loving wife and two healthy boys in a Christian home in Tennessee. He also leads and conducts the operations of multiple business ventures focused on firearms maintenance, and his consulting firm serves the Department of Defense with combat infantry training in various combat scenarios. It is his pleasure to pull from his life experiences and author this guidebook to help you prepare and address the realities of defending your home in a grid-down situation.